Prejudice

Tish Davidson

Franklin Watts
A Division of Scholastic Inc.
New York • Toronto • London • Auckland • Sydney
Mexico City • New Delhi • Hong Kong
Danbury, Connecticut

Dedication

For my husband, Scott

Cover illustration by Peter Cho.
Cover and interior design by Kathleen Santini.
Illustrations by Pat Rasch.

Library of Congress Cataloging-in-Publication Data

Davidson, Tish.
  Prejudice / Tish Davidson.
     p. cm. — (Life balance)
Includes bibliographical references and index.
  ISBN 0-531-12252-2 (lib. bdg.)   0-531-15572-2 (pbk.)
  1. Prejudices—Juvenile literature. 2. Hate—Juvenile literature.
3. Discrimination—Juvenile literature. I. Title. II. Series.
  BF575.P9D38 2003
  303.3'85—dc21

                                   2003000557

Table of Contents

One

What Is Prejudice?

On September 15, 2001, Balbir Singh Sodhi was at work in his gas station near Phoenix, Arizona. Like many immigrants that week, Sodhi was a little nervous. Just a few days earlier, right after hijacked planes destroyed the World Trade Center in New York, an angry man walked into the gas station and threatened him. Sodhi reported the threats to the police, but he was still worried that his appearance would make him a target for the pain and frustration Americans felt after the September 11 terrorist attacks.

Balbir Singh Sodhi was a Sikh. Sikhism *(seek-ism)* is a religion that was founded about five hundred years ago in northern

India. As part of their religious tradition, many Sikh men wear turbans and beards. Sikhism is not related to Islam, the religion of the September 11 hijackers. However, Sodhi's dress reminded many people of pictures they had seen of Osama bin Laden, the man suspected of planning the terrorist attacks.

Shortly after two o'clock, Sodhi went outside the gas station. A pickup truck pulled up. The driver fired several shots, and Sodhi fell dead. A few days later, the police arrested forty-two-year-old Frank Roque. They linked Roque to the murder of Sodhi and to the attempted murder of a Lebanese American and a family from Afghanistan. "I am a patriot! I'm an American. Arrest me and let those terrorists run wild," Roque was reported to have screamed when he was arrested.

Sadly, Roque had a twisted idea of patriotism that caused him to take his fear and anger out on innocent people. "Mr. Sodhi was apparently killed for no other reason than because he was dark-skinned, bearded, and wore a turban. He was killed because of hate," concluded Rick Romley, the county attorney.

Fortunately, few of us will ever experience the kind of prejudice, stereotyping, and hatred that leads to murder. However, we will meet people who do not know us but who will think or act negatively toward us because of the color of our skin, our age, sex, accent, sexual orientation, religious practices, income, appearance, or mental abilities. It is troubling that such prejudiced reactions are common in a nation built on the dreams of people from many lands, a nation that prides itself on its tolerance of differences.

Population of the United States by Race

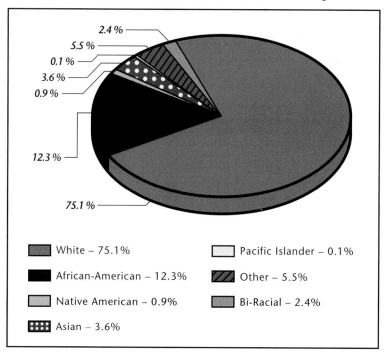

Racial minorities make up one-quarter of the population of the United States. Although Latinos make up 12.5% of the population, they are an ethnic group and are counted in the graph under the primary race by which they identify themselves. (Source: U.S. Census Bureau, 2000.)

What is prejudice? Where does it come from? Are all people prejudiced? How should we react when someone stereotypes us? Most importantly, what can we do to reduce prejudice and stereotyping? These are all questions we will explore in the following pages.

From Emotions to Action

"Don't judge a book by its cover" is a common saying. Logically, we know that we can't tell from looking at the outside of a book if we will enjoy reading it. The only way to know is to open the book and find out what is inside. Yet often we choose a book in the library or at a bookstore because the cover makes us think it will be interesting. In fact, to sell their products many advertisers encourage us to make snap judgments like this that are based on feelings, not facts.

The same thing happens when we meet people for the first time. Far too often we make quick judgments about what people are like based on their skin color, clothes, ethnic background, age, occupation, or even height and weight. This evaluation may happen so fast that we are not even aware of making it. These feelings of like or dislike made without basis in fact are called prejudices. Prejudice, or prejudgment, is usually not a thought-out decision. Although prejudices can be positive, the word is usually associated with negative reactions. Another word for prejudice is bias.

Prejudice starts as an emotion. The most common kind of prejudice is unconscious prejudice where people are not aware that they are making emotional judgments about other people. Unconscious prejudice often results in unintentionally prejudiced actions. People who are unintentionally prejudiced do not realize that they are doing something that hurts or offends someone else. A smaller number of people have well-developed, conscious prejudices. They are aware of their biases and know that when they express their prejudice it hurts others.

The presence of prejudice often leads to stereotyping. Stereotyping is viewing an entire group of people in a single way without considering individual differences. People who accept stereotypes as true make broad statements such as "teenagers are troublemakers" or "rich people are snobs." These people believe that their judgments are based on facts. In reality, they have taken a few bits of information or a single experience and incorrectly applied this information to an entire group.

One result of stereotyping is to encourage people to divide humankind into "us" and "them." Once these categories are in place, it is easy to deny another person's spirit, individuality, and humanity. This process is called dehumanization. If people are seen as interchangeable objects, their needs and feelings can be ignored.

When people no longer recognize the humanity in other people, it is easy to treat them differently. Discrimination is the act of treating people unjustly simply because of their membership in a group. It is the final, visible result of prejudice, stereotyping, and dehumanization.

"The ignorant are always prejudiced and the prejudiced are always ignorant."
—Charles Victor Roman,
African-American doctor

From Prejudice to Discrimination

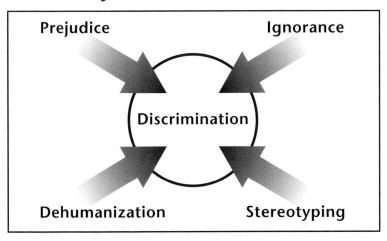

Prejudice	Ignorance
Discrimination	
Dehumanization	Stereotyping

Emotions, beliefs, and attitudes all can cause discrimination.

Why Prejudice Matters

Prejudices matter because they change our behavior. In 1968 Robert Rosenthal, a Harvard professor, and Leonore Jacobson, a San Francisco elementary-school principal, conducted a famous experiment on prejudice. They told one teacher that tests given at the start of the school year had identified some of her students as ready to excel academically. In fact, the students labeled as potential high achievers were chosen at random and had no greater academic abilities or potential than the rest of the class. However, because the teacher expected these students to do exceptionally well, they did. When tested again at the end of the school year, the chosen students improved their test scores more than the rest of the class.

Once some students were labeled as high achievers, the teacher developed expectations for them. Their role was to be the smart kids and succeed in school. The chosen students fulfilled their role and did succeed. Remember that the teacher's judgment of these students was based only on what she had been told, not on her own observations or any information that she had gathered herself. Even so, her expectations became a self-fulfilling prophecy: What she believed was true became true.

Why did the chosen students improve their test scores more than the students who were not labeled high achievers? It was not because they were smarter than their classmates. More likely, the teacher unconsciously changed her teaching style to give these students more time, attention, and support. She may have set higher academic expectations for them, showed that she had more confidence in their ability to learn, or been more careful to answer their questions and make sure they understood the material. Ultimately, the teacher's prejudice changed her behavior.

How We Interpret Events

The prejudices we carry with us also unconsciously affect our understanding of things that happen around us. They may make it hard to accept the views of people who are different from us. They can also keep us from reaching agreement about the meaning of an event. After a race-related murder in Jasper, Texas, two filmmakers wanted to explore this topic and made a documentary showing how prejudices and stereotyping cause people to view the same event differently.

Jasper is a town of 7,500 people. It is about 55 percent white and 45 percent black. On the night of June 6, 1998, James Byrd Jr., a middle-aged African American man, hitched a ride in a pickup truck with three white men. He never made it home. The men drove to an isolated spot and beat up Byrd. Next they chained him to the truck and dragged him more than 3 miles (4.8 kilometers), until he died and his body was torn apart. This brutal crime shocked the community. The murderers were caught, and two of them were sentenced to death. The third received a sentence of life in prison.

Whitney Dow, a white filmmaker, is a friend of Marco Williams, an African American filmmaker. As they talked about what had happened in Jasper, Dow said they realized that "we had a lot of divergent [different] thoughts and ideas about what the crime meant, based on the fact that Marco's black and I'm white." As a result, they decided to take two film crews, one African American and one white, to Jasper. The crews interviewed people of their own race about Byrd's death. The resulting film, *Two Towns of Jasper,* showed many of the underlying prejudices and stereotypes that caused whites and African Americans to have different views of the crime.

The filmmakers found that white people saw Byrd's murder as an isolated incident. It was a shocking, extraordinary event, but an event that they could never imagine would happen to them, and one that they did not fear would be repeated. Generally, the white people interviewed played down the importance of race in the murder and were quick to stereotype Byrd by pointing out his flaws. One white woman in the film says, "You know, I thought he spent most of his time in jail ... I want the defense [lawyers for the three men accused of the murder] to come out and tell who James Byrd was and what he was like, 'cause James Byrd wasn't the pillar of the community that they have made him out to be." This speaker seems to suggest that Byrd's supposed character flaws caused his murder, despite the fact that he did nothing to provoke his attackers.

African Americans in Jasper were also horrified by the murder, but they were not surprised. They saw Byrd's death as part of a continuing pattern of brutal racial discrimination, oppression, and hate that they had all experienced.

They identified strongly with Byrd and believed that they could easily become the next murder victim. In the film, one African American woman says, "Everybody says it's an isolated incident. It is not. It has been going on for quite a while." Another says she is afraid. "You're always looking over your shoulder."

The film *Two Towns of Jasper* shows how our life experiences act as filters through which we understand the world. The people of Jasper interviewed in the film agreed on the facts of James Byrd's murder. But each group interpreted the facts through its own prejudices and stereotypes to arrive at different conclusions about what his murder meant to them and to their town. So where did these prejudices and stereotypes come from, and how did they feed an irrational hate that ended in murder?

Two

The Roots of Prejudice

Ahmed and Sanjay were fourth graders in Mrs. Wright's class in Fremont, California. Ahmed and his family are Muslims who came to California from Pakistan. Sanjay and his family are Hindus from India. India and Pakistan have a long history of political and religious disagreement.

When it came time to assign students to reading groups, Wright put Sanjay and Ahmed at the same table.

Sanjay was angry. "I can't work with him," he said, pointing at Ahmed.

"Why not?" asked Wright.

"He's from Pakistan. Everybody knows that people from India don't talk to people from Pakistan."

"I don't want to work with him, either," said Ahmed. "I don't like Indians."

"Just a minute," said Wright. "I know that you come from countries that don't always get along, but you are in the United States now. It is time to leave those ideas behind. There are children in this classroom from many different countries. In America, we work together."

Although Ahmed and Sanjay stayed in the same reading group, they never cooperated, and their hostility flared up many times throughout the year. Even though they were only fourth graders, the prejudices they had brought with them from their home countries were too strong for them to put aside. Thinking about it later, Wright said, "I now realize that I wasn't going to be able to change generations of hostility in one year. The best that I could do was to give the boys a small experience of working with each other that might start a tiny crack in the prejudice that had been passed on to them."

(Ahmed, Sanjay, and Wright, like the other people in this book, are real people and this event actually happened. Their names have been changed to protect their privacy.)

Looking into the Brain

Ahmed and Sanjay were aware of their prejudices and expressed them clearly. Many of us, however, believe that we do not have prejudices. Although we may think that we do not make emotional prejudgments, the truth is that all of us except babies have prejudices. People who say, "I'm not prejudiced" may be completely unaware of their snap judgments, unconscious preferences, and biases.

For many years, social scientists have tried to understand the roots of prejudice in order to eliminate it. They have developed questionnaires to detect both obvious and hidden biases. They have observed and recorded behaviors that result from prejudice. In an effort to understand how prejudices affect the body, they have measured physical responses connected to emotions. For example, they can measure changes in blood pressure or eye movements when people are put in situations that might commonly cause a prejudiced response. However, until recently, social scientists lacked a way to see inside the brains of people during these situations.

Meanwhile, neurobiologists—scientists who study the nervous system—were studying the biology and chemistry of emotions. These scientists were interested in the physical changes that emotions cause in the brain. Around 1980, a technique called magnetic resonance imaging (MRI) was developed. MRI uses magnets, radio waves, and a computer to create three-dimensional pictures of soft tissue deep inside the body. It is especially useful for studying the brain.

When nerve cells (neurons) in the brain are stimulated, their chemistry changes. MRI can detect very small changes in brain chemistry, so by looking at MRI scans researchers can tell how many nerve cells are active. The first emotion neurobiologists studied was fear. They found that a scary situation increased the activity of nerve cells in a part of the brain called the amygdala (*ah-mig'-dah-la*).

The amygdala is a small, almond-shaped (the word *amygdala* comes from the Greek word for "almond") collection of nerve cells. There is one amygdala located on either side of the head, above the ear but deep inside the brain. After successfully studying fear, researchers began to look at moods and emotions such as love, pleasure, friendship, rage, and aggression. They discovered that all these feelings are produced and processed in the amygdala.

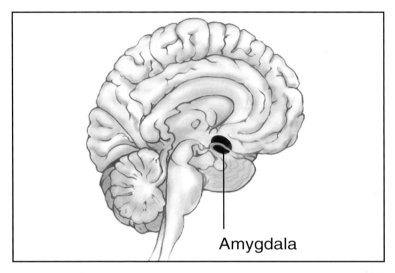

Amygdala

The amygdala is the place in the brain where emotions are processed.

After neurobiologists located the part of the brain that deals with emotions, psychologists decided to use MRI to study the role of the brain in prejudiced reactions. In one experiment, they gave white volunteers questionnaires to measure conscious prejudice and hidden prejudice. Next, they showed them pictures of unfamiliar African American and white men. As the volunteers looked at the pictures, an MRI scan recorded the activity in their amygdala.

The researchers found that when the white volunteers looked at African American faces, more nerve cells were active in the amygdala than when they looked at white faces. They also found that the higher people scored on hidden prejudice tests, the more active their amygdala was when they were shown African American faces.

At one time, these fear reactions may have helped people survive. Thousands of years ago, humans lived in tribes where most people were related to one another. They rarely met strangers, and when they did, these strangers were likely to be hostile. Being able to quickly categorize people as being like you (friend) or different from you (enemy) could be the difference between life and death.

Does this mean that we cannot do anything about our prejudices? No. In a second set of experiments, white volunteers were shown faces of well-known African American men who were positive role models—people such as Martin Luther King Jr. and Michael Jordan. When the volunteers looked at these familiar African American faces, their brain activity was the same as when they looked at white faces. This shows that our brains can change their response based on our life experiences.

Research into the role of biology in prejudice is still new, and there is disagreement among psychologists about how these brain reactions are related to actual stereotyping and discriminatory behavior. One suggestion, however, is that the better we get to know people who are different from us, the less likely it is that we will fear them, and when we are less fearful, we may have fewer unconscious or hidden prejudiced emotions.

Diversity on Television

Television and the movies have a long history of portraying different groups as stereotypes. For many years, the only movie roles open to African American actors were servants or cartoonlike entertainers. Asians were often shown as sneaky bad guys with funny accents, and Italians as gangsters. Physically handicapped people rarely appeared on television at all. Today, people of color are less stereotyped on television, but the number of roles for minority actors or actors with disabilities still remains small.

Unconscious Prejudice

Although biology may play a role in making quick prejudgments, most prejudice is learned unconsciously from those around us. This unconsciously learned prejudice affects our thoughts and actions in ways that we never even realize and often results in unintentional prejudiced actions. Unconsciously learned prejudices can even be the opposite of our conscious beliefs. This explains why many people who take tests to detect hidden prejudices have results that differ from the level of prejudice that they believe they have.

Children start absorbing prejudices unconsciously when they are very young. They hear how the people around them talk about others. They see how family members treat people of different races, religions, and social class. They notice how television, movies, and books show different groups. Gradually children accept certain ideas about whole groups of people as true before they are old enough to have any experience with individuals from these groups. As they grow, people rarely take time to think critically about these childhood "truths."

Even children as young as three or four years old can express unconsciously learned prejudices. One four-year-old

Attitude Adjustment

Social scientists at Yale University and the University of Washington have developed tests called implicit association tests to measure unconscious, automatic attitudes or biases. These tests calculate the difference in the time it takes you to respond to pairs of concept words, for example "young and pretty" or "old and pretty." The theory is that when you have the habit of thinking that two concepts go together, you respond faster when you see them paired. For example, you would probably respond quicker to "ham and eggs" than "ham and beans." The difference in the time it takes to respond to pairs of concepts shows hidden biases.

You can take online tests to see if you have hidden prejudices at www.tolerance.org. Remember—almost everyone has some hidden prejudices. By recognizing them, you can begin to consciously change your attitudes.

was overheard telling her five-year-old neighbor, "You're stupid because you don't go to private school." She is expressing a prejudice that she probably picked up from her family or school friends.

Unintentional prejudice can take many forms. In April 2002, the clothing manufacturer Abercrombie & Fitch introduced some T-shirts for teenagers. One shirt showed two Asian men with slanted eyes and conical hats. The logo read "Wong Brothers Laundry Service. Two Wongs can make it white." The shirts made some shoppers angry because they thought they were racist.

A spokesperson for Abercrombie & Fitch told the press that the shirts were "in no way intended to offend anyone" but were intended to be amusing and "add humor" to the clothing. "Everyone here at the company thought it was funny. I even polled Asians around the office today of what they thought of the shirts, and they thought the shirts were hilarious," said the Abercrombie & Fitch representative.

But other people saw no humor in the shirts. "It is really disappointing because the T-shirts make fun of nearly everything about our culture: our language, our religious beliefs, our occupations," said Cindy Liu, a Chinese American from San Jose, California. Asians were not the only ones who found the clothing insulting. Complaints from shoppers forced the company to remove the shirts from stores. With millions of dollars at stake, Abercrombie & Fitch had not intended to insult Asians, but their lack of awareness resulted in a costly public display of unintentional prejudice.

Unconscious prejudice is like a computer program that is always running in the background. We are not often aware of what it is doing, but it can have great effects. Our unconscious prejudices cause us unknowingly to develop expectations that everyone in a particular group will act in a certain way—for example that tall African American men will be good basketball players, Asian Americans will be good at math and science, girls won't want to take auto shop in school, men don't teach kindergarten, and teenagers are irresponsible and can't be trusted. These role expectations create stereotypes.

Stereotypes are learned judgments that result in a single way of viewing a group of people. Stereotyping does not allow for individual differences, and since every person's

"If we were to wake some morning and find that everyone was the same race, creed, and color, we would find some other causes for prejudice by noon."
—George Aiken,
United States Senator

genetic makeup and life experiences are different, stereotypes are most often wrong.

Language Prejudice?

Many words have meanings rooted in stereotypes. For example to gyp (cheat) someone comes from the word gypsy. The stereotype of a gypsy is someone who will cheat or take unfair advantage whenever possible. The offensive expression "jew somebody down" means to bargain hard to get a lower price. This expression is rooted in the stereotype that all Jewish people are cheapskates who are aggressive about trying to get a bargain. "Going Dutch" is a date where each person pays for him- or herself. The phrase refers to the stereotype that Dutch people are so tightfisted with their money that they will not treat someone else to an outing.

When people are assigned to categories based on stereotypes, it is easier to treat them as objects rather than as human beings. Once people are seen as objects, their needs and feelings can be ignored. This results in dehumanization.

What happens when a group of good people is given total control over another group of people much like themselves in an environment that encourages stereotyping and dehumanization? This was a question Philip Zimbardo, a psychology professor at Stanford University in Palo Alto,

California, wanted to answer. In an experiment conducted in 1971, he converted a Stanford building to look like a prison. College-aged volunteers were randomly divided into "guards" and "prisoners." The prisoners were picked up at their homes by the Palo Alto police and brought to the "jail." Here the dehumanization process began as they were stripped naked, sprayed with insecticide, given a prison uniform, and assigned a number instead of a name.

The volunteers chosen as guards had almost total power over the prisoners but received no instructions on how to run the prison. Soon the guards were harassing and humiliating the prisoners. By the second day, the prisoners started a rebellion. The guards used physical force to stop it, spraying the prisoners with fire extinguishers. They also withdrew prisoner privileges and used psychological strategies to make the prisoners fight among themselves.

Within thirty-six hours, prisoners started having psychological breakdowns. Emotionally, they believed that they were actual prisoners and could not leave the jail, even though logically they knew that they were just participating in a psychology experiment in a Stanford building.

During the next few days, the guards increased their physical and emotional punishment of the prisoners, especially when they thought no one was watching. They did not know that they were secretly being videotaped. The dehumanization process continued, as guards no longer saw the prisoners as students like themselves but as enemies to be controlled. Soon prisoners began to have serious psychological breakdowns. The guards became more violent. The experiment went completely out of control. Although the prisoners were supposed to stay in "jail" for fourteen days, the experiment was ended after the sixth day to protect the prisoners from abuse by the guards.

Keep in mind that all the people in this experiment were volunteers with similar backgrounds who knew that they were randomly picked to be either guards or prisoners. Despite this, almost immediately the guards used their power to stereotype, dehumanize, and violently discriminate against the prisoners. To learn more about this experiment, you can read Philip Zimbardo's day-by-day journal of the Stanford prison experiment at www.prisonexp.org.

The Anatomy of

Three

Discrimination

Rev. Matt Hale is proud to be a racist. Hale, a law school graduate, is the leader of the World Church of the Creator. This "church" calls its religion "Creativity" and claims to be "the fastest growing White racist and anti-Semite church in America." (An anti-Semite is a person who is prejudiced against Jews.)

Founded by Florida state legislator Ben Klassen in 1973, the World Church of the Creator claims to have 70,000 to 80,000 members in forty-eight states and twenty-eight countries. Its stated mission is "the Survival, Expansion, and Advancement of the White Race." Its slogan, RAHOWA, stands for *ra*cial *ho*ly *wa*r.

Hale travels around the United States taking advantage of the right of free speech to give talks such as "The Jew Is Through in 2002." He reaches other potential converts to his white supremacist organization through a Web site and with books by Klassen, such as *Nature's Eternal Religion* and *The White Man's Bible.*

Hale claims that his beliefs are based on "the lessons of history, on logic, and common sense." He says, "We [the World Church] regard the White Race as having risen to the very top of the human scale, with varying graduations of subhuman species [nonwhite races] below us." The World Church of the Creator is a hate group where prejudice is carried to violent extremes. Its followers have been convicted of the racially motivated murders of African Americans, Asian Americans, and Jews.

Intentional Prejudice

While everyone carries around unconscious prejudices, some people, like Hale, cultivate conscious and intentional prejudiced ideas. This conscious prejudice is much less common than unconscious, unintentional prejudice, but it is far more likely to lead to acts of discrimination and violence against people who are stereotyped as being in some way different.

Most people who say or do things because of unconscious prejudice are reacting out of thoughtlessness, habit, and ignorance. Although their words or actions may hurt, they are not acting out of planned meanness. On the other hand, people with conscious prejudices want to hurt others. They use their prejudices as weapons to build themselves up and tear others down. They often choose their targets and plan their actions in advance the same way bullies do. Another name for intentional prejudice is bigotry, and people who act with intentional prejudice are called bigots.

Studies have shown that bigots share certain characteristics. Most:

- have experienced a lot of physical punishment in childhood
- see human relationships in terms of control or power
- respect strong authority figures
- actively make their prejudiced beliefs part of their identity and lifestyle
- feel threatened by people who are different from them
- feel no guilt about their prejudiced actions

Conscious prejudices are learned later in life than unconscious prejudices. They are much more closely tied to a bigot's sense of identity and affect the person's entire view of the world. It is very difficult to change the behavior of a bigot.

A Comparison of Intentional and Unintentional Prejudices	
Person with Unintentional Prejudices	**Person with Intentional Prejudices**
Learned attitude early in life	Learned attitude later in life
Absorbed prejudices unconsciously from family, friends, and society	Actively learned prejudices from hate literature or other bigots
Does not plan prejudiced reactions; prejudiced responses often result from thoughtlessness	Spends time planning prejudiced actions with the intention of hurting others
Rarely spends much time thinking about stereotypes	Constantly thinks and talks about stereotypes; angry about minorities
May have unconscious prejudices that conflict with conscious beliefs about people	Prejudices are a major part of an identity and lifestyle
When accused of acting prejudiced, may deny it or feel guilty	When accused of acting prejudiced, may admit it proudly; no guilt, blames minorities for his or her misfortunes

A Comparison of Intentional and Unintentional Prejudices *(continued)*	
Person with Unintentional Prejudices	**Person with Intentional Prejudices**
Behavior can be changed by making the person aware that prejudicial response is hurtful	Very difficult to change; considers his or her behavior acceptable and feels threatened when asked to change

Discrimination: Prejudice in Action

Discrimination is the act of treating people unjustly because of their membership in a group. Prejudice, ignorance, fear, and envy are the main causes of discrimination. Until the 1960s, many people in the United States thought it was acceptable to openly discriminate against people whose appearance, abilities, or religion differed from the white, middle-class majority who ran the country. Immigrants, with their different languages, religions, and customs, often were—and still are—targets of discrimination.

In the past, individuals as well as institutions such as schools, the military, employers, and the government practiced open discrimination that in most cases was both legal and socially acceptable. For many people, the United States is the land of opportunity, but discrimination

Locking Up the "Enemy"

On December 7, 1941, in the midst of World War II, Japanese bombers attacked a U.S. naval base at Pearl Harbor in Hawaii. More than 2,400 Americans were killed. In response, the United States declared war on Japan and entered World War II, fighting on the side of England, France, and the Soviet Union.

At this time, about 125,000 people of Japanese ancestry lived in the United States. The United States government worried that people of Japanese descent might help the Japanese military attack the West Coast. The government directed the War Relocation Agency to round up people of Japanese ancestry, who were then held in internment camps away from the coast. This action was ordered even though there had been no acts against the United States by any Japanese Americans, nor any information to suggest that Japanese Americans would turn against the United States.

Japanese Americans were denied their civil rights and the protection the law gave other citizens simply because of prejudice and fear. For no reason other than their ethnicity, they were treated like criminals and held in internment camps for four years. In addition to losing their basic rights and freedoms, many families lost their homes and businesses.

In 1988, the U.S. Congress recognized the injustice of these actions and passed the Civil Liberties Act. This law authorized $20,000 and an official letter of apology for each person who had been held in an internment camp. Sadly, many of the people who had been in the camps had already died, and the money did not come close to fairly compensating those still alive for their losses.

against certain groups based on their race, religion, country of origin, sexual orientation, gender, social class, abilities, or other physical characteristics continues to be an ugly part of the American story.

Throughout the history of the United States, the most consistent acts of stereotyping, dehumanization, and discrimination have occurred against people of African ancestry. However, in the middle of the twentieth century, attitudes toward African Americans slowly began to change. Before that time, the practice of segregation kept whites and blacks in separate schools, separate military units, and separate neighborhoods. Although laws called for separate but equal treatment of the races, the results were anything but equal. White schools were better funded. White neighborhoods got better police and fire protection. White people held almost all the positions of economic and political power. They were the employers, the elected officials, the lawmakers, and the judges. Even in places where segregation was not the law, people of different races simply did not live and work together.

In 1951, in Topeka, Kansas, the policy of racial segregation in schools was challenged in the courts. The case, *Brown v. Board of Education,* reached the United States Supreme Court in 1954. The Court ruled, "To separate [African American children] from others of similar age and qualifications solely because of their race generates a feeling of inferiority as to their status in the community that may affect their hearts and minds in a way unlikely ever to be undone." The Court ordered an end to schools segregated by race.

> *"We hate some persons because we do not know them; and will not know them because we hate them."*
> *—Charles Caleb Colton,*
> *English minister and writer*

During the next ten years, the civil rights movement grew stronger as it struggled to bring legal, political, and social equality to all Americans. In 1964, the federal Civil Rights Act outlawed discrimination based on race, color, religion, gender, or national origin. This law did not end the practice of discrimination, however, because white people still held almost all the positions of power. Despite the actions of Congress, many people resisted examining their prejudices and changing the way they thought and acted toward minorities.

The Civil Rights Act, however, did give people who were discriminated against a way to legally challenge their treatment. Gradually other laws were passed to protect people from discrimination based on age, gender, sexual orientation, and disabilities. Although these laws have reduced open acts of discrimination, quiet discrimination still exists in many forms in the United States.

Hate Crimes

Laws provide ways to challenge discrimination when it happens, but they cannot force people to change their attitudes. Some bigots who hold strong prejudices continue to use open discrimination and violence against groups they detest. When a person commits a crime against someone because of the victim's race, ethnic origin, religion, or sexual orientation, that crime is called a hate crime. Many laws provide severe penalties for hate crimes.

People who hate sometimes come together with others who share their beliefs to form hate groups. Hate groups are not just an American problem. The Skinheads are an example of an international hate group. Skinheads are a white racist organization that attracts mainly alienated young men. They are against people of color, Jews, homosexuals, and immigrants. Skinheads use violence as a way of hurting, bullying, and intimidating the people they hate. Skinheads are neo-Nazis or "new Nazis." The original Nazi Party, led by Adolph Hitler in Germany in the 1930s and 1940s, believed in keeping the white race pure by killing Jews, gypsies, and people with mental or physical disabilities. Skinheads share this philosophy.

The Skinhead movement began in England in the 1970s. By the 1980s, they were an organized group of violent young men in their teens and twenties. They shaved their heads (giving them the name Skinheads); wore heavy boots, tattoos, and military clothing; and displayed their aggression by picking fights. Their leader in the 1980s, Ian Stuart, founded a band called Skrewdriver, whose music promoted white power and the hatred of minorities. Using music, the Internet, and hate literature to recruit new members, the Skinhead movement spread to the United States, Germany, Hungary, the Czech Republic, Poland, Brazil, Italy, Sweden, and Canada by the 1990s.

Like most hate groups, Skinheads are a small but violent organization. In the United States, they are believed to have committed at least twenty-five murders. In 1998, there were about 3,500 Skinheads active in forty states.

Reasons for Hate Crimes

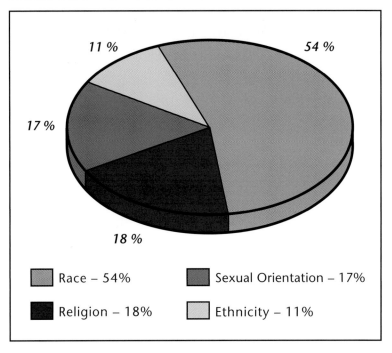

More than half the hate crimes committed in 1999 were motivated by racial prejudice. (Source: Federal Bureau of Investigation, 1999.)

Although hate groups are visible in their actions, most hate crimes are committed by people who do not belong to organized hate groups. Hate groups are legal, so long as they do not commit crimes. Their existence is the price Americans pay for the freedom to express their beliefs, no matter how ugly or unpopular.

Burning Crosses

One of the oldest hate groups in the United States is the Ku Klux Klan or KKK. The KKK was founded in 1865 in Tennessee by a group of angry Confederate (Southern) soldiers after the Civil War. Its mission was to destroy property and intimidate and murder people of color and those sympathetic to them. Its signature was a white hooded robe, a burning cross, and a noose for hanging.

Originally, members of the KKK turned their anger on African Americans, but over time they have come to hate other minority groups as well. The KKK is responsible for burning homes and schools, bombing businesses and voting places, and whipping, beating, and murdering people in almost every state. Klan membership reached a peak in the 1920s when 40,000 members marched in Washington, D.C. Today several thousand people still belong to the KKK.

Four

Prejudice in Action

Mark had always wanted to be a police officer. He joined the Minneapolis police department as soon as he graduated from college. He was one of the few African Americans on the force, but when he worked with other officers he never felt that his race was an issue. It was different, however, in the community.

One day, when he was off duty, Mark went to the Mall of America to buy a pair of jeans and some new shirts. As he moved through a department store selecting clothes that he wanted to try on, he became aware that a middle-aged man was following him. "This guy had 'store detective' written all over him," said Mark. "I should know, because one year during the holidays I worked mall security as a second job to make some extra money."

Finally, Mark had enough of being followed. He turned around to the man and said, "Hi, don't I know you from somewhere? I think we met last year when I was working security here at the mall and picked up a couple of shoplifters from your store." The store detective mumbled something about not recognizing Mark, then turned away.

"I put back the clothes I was going to try on and left the store," said Mark. "I haven't been back since. I'm not going to spend my money at a place that thinks just because I'm young and black, I'm a shoplifter."

Racial Profiling

Today many laws exist that are intended to protect people from discrimination. However, as Mark discovered when he went shopping, prejudice, stereotyping, and discrimination still happen daily. In Mark's case, the store detective was stereotyping Mark and using racial profiling to target him as a potential shoplifter because he was young and black.

Profiling involves targeting individuals for special scrutiny for no reason other than that they belong to a specific group. Law officers develop profiles by looking for certain characteristics or patterns of behavior that from past experience suggest someone may be involved in criminal activity. For example, if customs agents know that drug smugglers tend to follow certain travel patterns, they may search a high percentage of people whose travel fits those patterns, even if they have no other reason for suspecting that the travelers are smuggling drugs.

Racial profiling occurs when people of one race or ethnic group are examined more closely than everyone else simply because of their physical appearance. Some people think that including race or ethnicity in a criminal profile creates stereotypes that lead to discrimination and an abuse of power. They argue that by including race in a criminal profile, many innocent people of color are subjected to unreasonable harassment, even when there are no other reasons to think that they have done anything against the law.

Other people believe that it is just good sense to include race or ethnic appearance as part of a criminal profile. They argue that if past experience has shown that people of a particular racial or ethnic group are more likely to commit a crime, that is reason enough to give everyone who belongs to the group special scrutiny. Several factors must be considered in deciding when, if ever, racial profiling is a useful technique. These include the proportion of

members of the profiled group who are criminals, the like-
lihood of catching them by using profiling, the seriousness
of the crime being detected, the cost to the majority of the
profiled group who are innocent, and the cost to society of
continuing to emphasize racial and ethnic divisions.

Good Sense or Discrimination?

*After the terrorist attacks of September 11, 2001, screeners
at airport-security checkpoints began paying close attention
to passengers who looked like they were Arabs or Muslims,
because the terrorists had been Muslim men. They justified
their action on the grounds that Arab-looking men "fit the
profile" of the terrorists. As a result, many Middle Eastern
men were stopped and searched in airports. Some innocent
people were detained for many hours and missed their flights.*

*In a Knight Ridder poll, sixty-two percent of Americans
believed that security officials should pay special attention to
those who appeared to be Arab or Muslim. Is this good sense
or discrimination? You can learn more about profiling and
take a test to see if you can pick out the characteristics that
make up law enforcement's drug-smuggler profile by going
online to www.horizonmag.com/6/racial-profiling.asp.*

The Costs of Prejudice

Prejudice, stereotyping, dehumanization, and discrimination
have economic and social costs that affect people in both

obvious and hidden ways. Studies have documented discrimination in almost every aspect of life including:

- Employment—Interviews with job seekers whose race was different from that of the interviewer were shorter than when the interviewer and the job seeker were the same race.

- Housing—Seventy percent of the difference in approval rates for housing loans among different races could be accounted for by racial discrimination rather than credit rating or job history.

- Access to health care—Fewer African American women were referred for mammograms (tests to detect breast cancer) than white women, and yet African American women die of breast cancer at a higher rate than white women.

- Selective enforcement of laws—African American men made up only 5 percent of drivers on Interstate 95, but they accounted for 80 percent of drivers stopped by police officers on this highway.

Prejudice and the actions it causes also have emotional and psychological costs. Researchers have found that people who are physically attacked in a hate crime have more stressful emotional and psychological side effects than people who are attacked for other reasons, such as during a robbery. Depression, anger with family members, loss of friends, nervousness, withdrawal from social activities, difficulty working or studying, loss of self-confidence, and problems sleeping are common responses to hate-crime attacks.

People who are victims of a hate crime are more fearful, feel more vulnerable, and are more likely to believe that they cannot prevent bad things from happening to them because of society's prejudice toward them. Dr. Gregory Herek, a psychologist at the University of California-Davis who specializes in the psychological effects of hate crimes against homosexuals, said in a radio interview that his research data showed that "after about two years or so, the victims of non-hate crimes started to get back to normal, whereas the victims of hate crimes didn't. It took them longer."

A more subtle effect of bias is that the group targeted by a particular prejudice begins to act the way its members are stereotyped. For example, African American boys are often stereotyped as people with great athletic ability but few book smarts. It isn't just the white majority who believe this stereotype. Studies have shown that many African Americans also see themselves that way. As a result, among some African American students, it is considered, "too white" to do well in school. In order to fit in socially, some academically talented African American boys feel pressured to hide their intelligence and conform to the expectation that they are poor students.

Discrimination and the Law

For many years, open discrimination against women and minorities was written into the law. Before the civil rights movement of the 1960s, white men controlled almost every aspect of economic and political power in the United States. In the South, laws known as Jim Crow laws were designed to keep African Americans from fully participating in social, economic, and political life.

Constitutional Discrimination

Even in the United States, which was founded on the principle that "all men are created equal," equality was originally meant to apply only to white men. The fifteenth amendment to the U.S. Constitution says, "The right of citizens of the United States to vote shall not be denied or abridged by the United States or by any State on account of race, color, or previous condition of servitude [slavery]." This amendment was not ratified until 1870, eighty-three years after the Constitution was adopted. Before then, only white men could vote. Women were not allowed to vote for another fifty years, until the nineteenth amendment was ratified in 1920.

Today, as a result of the civil rights movement, many laws are in place to protect people who are discriminated against. To be protected from discrimination, a person

Finding a Balance: Affirmative Action

Affirmative action is a concept that was developed by the federal government starting in the 1960s. Affirmative-action programs attempt to make up for years of discrimination against certain racial minorities by considering race in situations such as hiring or promoting workers or admitting students to universities. Some of the first affirmative-action programs set aside a specific number of jobs, called a quota, that could only be filled by minorities that had been historically discriminated against.

White student Allan Bakke had been rejected twice from the University of California-Davis Medical School. He took the university to court, claiming that he had been discriminated against because of his race. At that time, the UC-Davis affirmative-action program set aside sixteen of the one hundred places in each medical school class for minority students. Minority applicants competed only against each other for these sixteen spots, while white applicants competed against each other for the remaining spaces. The separate consideration of white and racial-minority applicants led to the admission of some minority students who had lower test scores and grades than rejected white applicants like Bakke. Bakke claimed that this was racial discrimination because ability alone should be the basis for admission to medical school.

The lawsuit went to the U.S. Supreme Court, where in 1978 the Court ruled that it was in the best interest of society to admit a diverse student body to university programs. Race, they said, could be considered only as one factor among many—including grades, test scores, extracurricular activities, and family hardships—in selecting students for admission. However, setting aside a fixed number of spaces or a quota only for selected racial minorities was illegal.

This ruling did not end affirmative action. However, it failed to make clear exactly how race should be a factor in admissions. In December 2002, the U.S. Supreme Court again agreed to hear two cases involving affirmative action. In both these cases, white students accused the University of Michigan of using a race-based standard that allowed them to reject more qualified white applicants, while at the same time admitting less qualified people of color. (When this book went to press, these cases had not yet been decided.)

must belong to a group called a protected class. Protected classes are based on race, color, national origin, gender, religion, disability, or age. Many states and cities have passed laws that create other protected classes of people based on characteristics such as marital status or sexual orientation.

The law does not protect everyone who is discriminated against. For example, people who smoke or who own pets are not considered part of a protected class, so landlords may legally refuse to rent to them. On the other hand, a

> *"You do not take a man who for years has been hobbled by chains, liberate him, bring him to the starting line of a race, saying, 'you are free to compete with all the others,' and still believe that you have been completely fair."*
> *—Lyndon Johnson,*
> *36th U.S. president*

landlord may not refuse to rent to a family simply because it is Latino. This would be discriminating against the family members based on their ethnicity. The landlord could, however, refuse to rent to a Latino family that has bad credit. The difference is that, in the first case, the family was rejected because of prejudice against Latinos.

In the second case, the reason for the rejection was that the family's bad credit made it a poor business risk. This is not discrimination if the landlord also refuses to rent to whites, African Americans, and Asian Americans with similar credit histories.

Even though laws exist to protect people from discrimination, acts of discrimination can be hard to prove in court. Many successful cases that go to court show a pattern of discriminatory actions against an individual or a protected class of people. The laws against discrimination are constantly being challenged in the courts as our understanding of what is fair and equal treatment evolves.

Five

Fighting Discrimination

anukkah (*ha'-neh-ka*) is a Jewish holiday that celebrates the rededication of the Temple in Jerusalem after a period when Jews were prevented from practicing their religion. For eight nights in December 1993, the Schnitzer family of Billings, Montana, celebrated Hanukkah as they always did by lighting candles and placing them in a menorah (*meh-noor'-a*) in their window. On the third night of Hanukkah, someone tossed a rock through the Schnitzers' window where their menorah blazed. This was one of a series of hate crimes against Jews, Native Americans, and African Americans in Billings. Although the police had taken these incidents seriously, they had not been able to catch the people responsible for them.

The Schnitzer family was frightened, but they refused to be intimidated into taking down their menorah. Then a Christian minister suggested a way to protect the Schnitzers and to demonstrate that the town rejected the prejudices of the rock throwers. Religious leaders encouraged people of all faiths to display a menorah. Sunday-school classes made menorahs. Women's groups made menorahs. The local paper printed a full-page picture of a menorah for people to tape in their windows. Soon there were menorahs in ten thousand homes all over Billings. By identifying themselves with a group the rock throwers hated, the people of Billings made a statement that they would not accept prejudice and hatred in their town.

What if I Am a Target of Prejudice?

Prejudice and discrimination are problems in every country and every culture. Sooner or later, you will be the target of prejudice. It can be as simple as someone assuming that you fit a stereotype or as ugly as being beaten up because you look different from those around you. When you experience prejudice and discrimination, you will probably feel humiliated, angry, scared, and hurt. Before you respond, you need to get your emotions under control.

Answering prejudice with prejudice only increases hostility and disrespect.

Suppose that someone starts telling jokes that disrespect your ethnic group and make people like you look stupid. How can you make it clear that you find these jokes prejudiced and not funny? First, you can simply walk away. A joke needs an audience to get a laugh. If the prejudiced comments continue, you might decide to say something.

Speaking out is a good thing to do because people often are unaware that their words are hurtful or biased. They simply don't think about what they are saying or are mindlessly repeating what they have heard others say. Letting them know that their words are unacceptable to you may help them to stop, think, and change. Unfortunately, sometimes when students speak out against prejudice at school, they become the target of hateful comments. If this happens, tell a teacher or other responsible adult. Schools have rules that can be used to stop harassment, bullying, and the use of hate words.

If you choose to confront a prejudiced person about his or her words, use an "I" message, not a "you" message. For example, say "I think that joke is insulting, not funny," rather than "You shouldn't tell a joke like that." The person you challenge may feel uncomfortable and accuse you of being too sensitive or of overreacting. Remember that you always have a right to your own feelings.

Each situation is different. For example, if someone makes a classroom poster that you think is sexist, you might choose to tell the teacher how you feel rather than confronting the poster maker. The teacher can then bring up the subject of sexism and respect to the entire class. Learning to state your feelings when you are the target of prejudice without becoming angry or using ugly, prejudiced words yourself sends a message that you are serious about discrimination. It also increases your self-respect.

When No Response Is the Best Response

Imagine this scene: You start to cross the street on the green light, when a car coming the other way runs the red light and comes roaring through the intersection. You have the right of way, and the car running the red light is in the wrong. But you jump back on the curb because staying safe is more important than insisting on your right to cross the street.

If you face people who are so bigoted or a situation so tense that responding may start a fight or cause people to get hurt, it is time to "jump back on the curb." You know that these people are wrong, but your safety is more important than insisting on your rights. Instead, report the event to a concerned adult or to the police.

Since the passage of the Hate Crimes Act, law officers tend to treat seriously acts of prejudice, especially those associated with threats of violence. Hate crimes against property, such as hate graffiti, should also be reported. The American Civil Liberties Union (ACLU), the Southern Poverty Law Center, and similar organizations provide free or low-cost legal assistance to those who are discriminated against and whose civil rights are violated. When faced with a hate-crime situation, it is better to use the law to get justice than to try to reason with a bigot.

Standing Up to Prejudice

Taking a stand against prejudice is often easier and more effective for a person who sees but is not the target of a prejudiced act. You can speak up if you hear an ethnic joke and say, "I don't think that is funny." If someone makes a stereotyped comment such as "Girls are bad at math," you can disagree.

Another way to speak out against prejudice is to do or say something that identifies you with the target group, even though you belong to a different group. The people of Billings did this when they put menorahs in their windows even though some were not Jewish. By identifying with the target group, you help deflect the prejudice directed at it. The closer your relationship to the person with the prejudice, the greater effect your comments and actions will have. Friends do influence each other's thinking.

Speaking up when you see prejudice can be difficult, but staying silent helps prejudice and discrimination grow. Your silence encourages prejudiced people to believe that what they are doing is okay. A famous quotation by Martin Niemoeller, a Christian pastor and anti-Nazi activist in Germany during World War II, explains what happens if people remain silent when they know others are being discriminated against:

> First they came for the Communists, but I was not a Communist so I did not speak out. Then they came for the Socialists and the Trade Unionists, but I was neither, so I did not speak out. Then they came for the Jews, but I was not a Jew so I did not speak out. And when they came for me, there was no one left to speak out for me.

One of the best ways to break down prejudice is to work on a project or play on a sports team with people from different backgrounds. In 1961, psychologists designed an experiment where they created hostility by spreading ugly rumors and creating unnecessary competition between two similar groups of boys at a camp. Soon the groups started food fights and began name-calling, pushing, and shoving each other. One group burned the other group's banner.

Next, the researchers tried to reduce the anger and prejudice by having the groups share fun activities such as movies, picnics, and sporting events. This idea failed completely, and the two groups got into fistfights. Finally, although the boys did not know it, the psychologists set up "emergencies" where the two groups had to work together to solve a problem that affected them all. For example, they had to fix a break in the camp's water-supply line or the camp would shut down, and they would be sent home. Later they had to cooperate to get the food truck out of a ditch.

"Race prejudice...is a shadow over us all, and the shadow is darkest over those who feel it least and allow its evil effects to go on."
—Pearl Buck,
American novelist

When boys from both groups worked together on something important, positive feelings of respect and understanding developed between them. Their group identities became less important, and they stopped seeing each other as the enemy. Simply spending time together was not enough. For the change to take place, they had to work together for a common goal on a project that they all thought was important.

Face to Face

Seeds of Peace Camp in Otisfield, Maine, brings together students from areas of the world where there is conflict and violence. These teens come to the camp with strong prejudices and stereotypes acquired from their families and their cultures. At the camp, they work, live, and play together. They also learn how to communicate in ways that reduce tension and conflict. In explaining how he was changed by the camp, Jawad Issa, a Palestinian Arab, said, "In the Middle East, you don't see a face to the person on the other side. I realized [after attending Seeds of Peace] that there is a person behind the label Israeli. It surprised me that they were people I could like."

What if I Am Prejudiced?

Just realizing that you have picked up unconscious prejudices and biased attitudes before you were old enough to think them through is the first step in eliminating these prejudices. Look honestly at your attitudes. Do you feel uncomfortable about some of your stereotypes? Then make a commitment to consciously challenge your prejudices. Here are some things that can help you meet that commitment:

- Learn about people who are different from you through books, movies, and cultural events.

- Join a group that is committed to bringing about equality for all. It is easier to change if you are supported by others who share your commitment.
- When you are aware that you are responding to a person in a prejudiced or stereotyped way, consciously replace your mental image of that person with a positive and pleasant image.
- Start or join a multicultural group that is working toward a common goal.
- Look for common interests that you share with others regardless of their backgrounds.
- Learn how other people see the groups that you belong to. You are not the only one with prejudices.
- Participate in activities that make you feel good about yourself. People who feel positive about themselves are more secure and feel less of a desire to put others down.
- Work on developing empathy. Take time to consciously imagine what it would be like to walk in other people's shoes.
- Practice active listening skills so that you hear what is really being said, rather than what you expect to hear. You don't have to agree with everything that is said, but be open to hearing what others think.
- Learn and practice conflict-mediation skills. The

more resources you have to defuse prejudice, the more effective you will be.

- Support organizations in your school and community that teach respect, understanding, and tolerance. Put their teachings into practice in your life.
- Take responsibility for helping others when they are the target of prejudice and discrimination.
- Take responsibility for reporting hate crimes to the appropriate authorities.

Keep It Cool

Conflict resolution is a way of peacefully ending arguments that might otherwise lead to violence. Some schools offer special classes to train students in conflict resolution so that they can help their classmates solve everyday disputes. Conflict mediators learn ways to improve communication between the people having the dispute. They do not take sides or decide who is right or wrong. Instead, they listen to both sides, encourage them to explain their views to each other, and help to work out solutions that seem fair to both parties.

Prejudice, stereotyping, and discrimination are not just modern American problems. Prejudice has been a cause of oppression, wars, and death in every society in every country since the beginning of recorded history.

Much of the fighting that occurs in the world today is rooted in racial, religious, and economic prejudice and discrimination. There are no quick or easy solutions to creating equal respect and equal treatment for all people. Although laws can punish discriminatory behavior, they cannot change people's hearts. The only way to do that is to help people see beyond the labels and categories that are defined by prejudice and to recognize the humanity of every individual.

Nobel Peace Prize winner Nelson Mandela, who spent more than twenty-five years in prison in South Africa for fighting a political system that kept blacks and whites separate and unequal, expressed this idea in his autobiography, *Long Walk to Freedom.* He wrote,

It was during those long and lonely years [in prison] that my hunger for freedom of my own people became a hunger for the freedom of all people, white and black … A man who takes away another man's freedom is a prisoner of hatred; he is locked behind the bars of prejudice and narrow-mindedness. I am not truly free if I am taking away someone else's freedom, just as surely as I am not free when my freedom is taken from me. The oppressed and the oppressor alike are robbed of their humanity.

Glossary

aggravated assault: a violent, armed attack

amygdala: the part of the brain where emotions, especially fear and anxiety, are processed

anti-Semite: a person who is prejudiced against, has hostility toward, or discriminates against Jews

bigotry: intentional or consciously expressed prejudice; a person who is intentionally prejudiced is called a bigot

civil rights: the rights of all citizens to political, legal, and social equality

civil rights movement: an American social and political movement, originally dominated by African Americans, that works to bring equality to people of all races, religions, and ethnic and other minority groups

dehumanization: the process of denying a person's spirit, personality, individuality, and humanity

discrimination: the act of treating people differently because of their membership in a group; most discrimination is based on race, religion, ethnic origin, age, gender, sexual orientation, or disability

empathy: the ability to be aware of and sensitive to the thoughts, feelings, and experiences of others

ethnicity: a person's cultural background

gender: sex, either female or male

hate crime: an illegal act against people or property that is motivated by prejudice hate group: an organization of people who share the same prejudiced attitudes and who openly display those attitudes through hate literature, marches, rallies, and hate crimes

integration: people of different races having equal access to the same schools, stores, restaurants, and similar facilities

internment camps: eleven bases in the western United States where people of Japanese descent were imprisoned because of their ethnic background from 1942 until 1945, when World War II ended

prejudice: a prejudgment made with little thought or basis in fact

segregation: the act of keeping different groups separate from each other based on their race, religion, ethnic heritage, or similar characteristics

stereotypes: learned judgments that create a single way of viewing an entire group of people without regard to their individuality

Further Resources

Books

Able, Deborah. *Hate Groups,* Rev. ed. Berkeley Heights, N.J.: Enslow Publishers, Inc., 2000.
Looks at the roots of hate in America and why people commit hate crimes.

Bowman-Kruhm, Mary, and Claudine Wirths. *Coping with Discrimination and Prejudice.* New York: Rosen Publishing Group, 1998.
Broad review of discrimination with chapters devoted to different forms of discrimination.

Carnes, Jim. *Us and Them.* New York: Oxford University Press, 1996.
Engaging stories of real people who were involved in cases of discrimination and hate from 1660 to the present, with explanations to put these stories in perspective.

Engelbert, Phillis. *American Civil Rights: Primary Sources.* Detroit: UXL, 1999.
Excerpts from original writings by famous people on race with commentary ("what happened next").

Garg, Samidha, and Jan Hardy. *Racism.* Austin: Raintree Steck-Vaughn Co., 1997.
International perspective on racism for younger readers.

LaMachia, John. *So What Is Tolerance Anyway?* New York: Rosen Publishing Group, 2002.
Short book about discrimination, stereotypes, and tolerance.

Roleff, Tamara L., ed. *Extremist Groups: Opposing Viewpoints.* San Diego: Greenhaven Press, 2001.
Thought-provoking essays taking opposite points of view about the seriousness and effects of hate groups.

Turck, Mary C. *The Civil Rights Movement for Kids.* Chicago: Chicago Review Press, 2000.
A history of the civil rights movement with activities.

Williams, Mary E., ed. *Discrimination: Opposing Viewpoints.* San Diego: Greenhaven Press, 1997.
Essays taking opposite points of view about the effects of discrimination.

Online sites

Anti-Defamation League
www.adl.org
Information and lessons on prejudice and discrimination for teachers and parents.

Cole, Jim, Ed.D., "Beyond Prejudice"
www.eburg.com/~cole/index.html
Large Web site treating many aspects of prejudice, including remediation by an educator.

Simon Wiesenthal Center
motlc.wiesenthal.com/resources/
Site includes resources for educators, including suggested activities, lessons, and projects for teaching tolerance.

TeachersFirst.com
www.teachersfirst.com/lessons/terrorism.html
Lesson plans for teachers about tolerance, and information for students related to the terrorist attacks of September 11, 2001. Many links to other Web sites.

Tolerance.org, Southern Poverty Law Center

www.tolerance.org

This Web site offers material to get parents, teachers, and kids thinking about ways to expand the practice of tolerance in daily life. An extensive resource on prejudice, discrimination, and tolerance.

Related Organizations

American Civil Liberties Union (ACLU)

125 Broad Street, 18th Floor

New York, NY 10004

www.aclu.org

National organization with many state and local chapters devoted to protecting the rights of all people through legal action and education.

The National Conference for Community and Justice

475 Park Avenue South, 19th Floor

New York, NY 10016

www.nccj.org

Organization that works to advocate and educate and to resolve conflict associated with discrimination and oppression.

The Prejudice Institute

2743 Maryland Avenue

Baltimore, MD 21218

www.prejudiceinstitute.org

Education and information about fighting prejudice.

Southern Poverty Law Center

400 Washington Ave.

Montgomery, AL 36104

www.tolerance.org

Nonprofit organization that provides information about civil rights and teaching tolerance. Its mission is to combat hate, intolerance, and discrimination through education and legal channels. The Web site has a special section for students.

Index

About the Author

Tish Davidson graduated from the College of William and Mary and from Dartmouth College with degrees in biology. For many years, she has written about social and medical topics. She especially enjoys making complex information understandable to young readers. Davidson lives in Fremont, California. This is her fourth book.